D1090439

THE BATSFORD COLOUR BOOK OF
Hampshire
and the Isle of Wight

Introduction and commentaries by
John Norwood

B. T. BATSFORD LTD   LONDON

First published 1975

Filmset by Servis Filmsetting Ltd, Manchester
Made and printed by
Leefung Asco Printers Ltd, Hong Kong
for the publishers
B. T. Batsford Ltd, 4 Fitzhardinge Street, London W1H 0AH
ISBN 0 7134 3011 7

Contents

Acknowledgments

The Publishers wish to thank the following for permission to reproduce the photographs in this book:

British Travel Association, for page 55
J. Allan Cash, for page 23
Noel Habgood, for pages 19, 27, 43, 51
A. F. Kersting, for pages 39, 47, 61
Picturepoint, for pages 25, 49, 57
Kenneth Scowen, for pages 21, 29, 31, 33, 35, 41, 45, 53, 59, 63
Spectrum, for pages 17, 37

The Author wishes to thank Messrs S. R. Davey, J. H. Lavender and M. Ware for their help during preparation of the text.

Introduction

If one were asked what it was that made Hampshire different from other counties it would be difficult to give a neat answer, for it has neither the homogeneity of a geographical region such as the Fens or the Cotswolds, nor any clearly-defined boundaries other than the coast and the dotted line on the map. What it does possess are the important centres of Winchester and Southampton which act like two valves at the heart of the county's life and encourage in its people a sense of belonging. Hampshire people will tell you that it is a good county to live in, a belief which seems to be borne out by the numbers of newcomers who flock in, mainly to the south. Of course, other counties are agreeable, but not many offer such a wide range of attractions as does Hampshire: beautiful scenery, seaside recreation, excellent urban facilities, good communications and a pleasant climate to crown them. It has, too, a wealth of interest in its natural history and its past, in its remains of early man and ancient monuments, in its associations with historical and literary figures. In short, Hampshire possesses enriching qualities which although not individually rare are here so abundantly gathered as to make it an outstanding county.

Looked at on the map Hampshire has a rather irregular squarish shape with a projection towards Dorset in the southwest. It is traversed by great highways running from London to the West country by way of Basingstoke, to Southampton docks by way of Winchester, and to Portsmouth by way of Petersfield. A particularly busy road runs along the coast from Chichester to Southampton on its way across the New Forest to Bournemouth (once part of Hampshire, but now, with Christchurch, lost to Dorset). Hampshire has to put up with a tremendous volume of traffic through being in the path of these lines of communication, but to balance the picture it is only fair to say that it also has plenty of quiet roads and green lanes where cycling and walking can still be an enjoyable way of seeing the best of the countryside.

The county's coastline could fairly be described as useful rather than striking. However, there are plentiful harbours and inlets which give it great advantages for both commercial and recreational seafaring and on most days the waters between the mainland and the Isle of Wight are busy with craft of every description from dinghies to container ships.

A common seaway is really all that the Isle of Wight shares with Hampshire, for despite the many occasions when the two are referred to in one breath the island is a separate county and guards its integrity most jealously. *Overners* crossing from the mainland soon sense the apartness of the islanders but enjoy the less intense pressure on space and life which they find there.

Coming from London by road or rail en route for Bournemouth you will cut right across the three principal types of scenery which comprise Hampshire, each of them closely related to the underlying geology. The first one will hardly be noticed, for it is a continuation of the sandy heathland country characteristic of large areas of neighbouring Surrey, edge of the great London Basin. In Hampshire this occupies a wedge-shaped part of the northeast, lying above a line joining Kingsclere and Basingstoke with Farnham in Surrey. It is poor land agriculturally, with an insatiable demand for enrichment as many a gardener has found to his cost. It grows heather and birch and there has been a good deal of coniferous planting. The best crop seems to be houses, planted within easy reach of London and the atomic research establishment over the border at Aldermaston, and of course, it makes ideal manoeuvring ground for the army. The military presence has been firmly entrenched in the northeast region for a long time and the result in too many places has been a dereliction of disused ranges and old hutments; happily the Ministry of Defence are now taking steps to tidy things up. Until quite recent years this countryside also supported various traditional craftsmen such as broomsquires (besom makers), hurdle makers and rake makers, but demand has lessened and other employment has become more attractive and today you will be lucky to come across the occasional broomsquire cutting birch.

Moving further now into the county you enter the landscape characteristic of its largest area, the Hampshire Downs. This rolling countryside forms part of one of England's largest chalk masses and links Salisbury

Plain with the South Downs. Driving down, say, the A30 you might get the impression that this was a plateau with few variations in height, but it is actually relieved by numerous valleys and some are quite steep-sided; the main road through Wherwell boasts a hairpin bend worthy of a mountain pass and there are some stiff hills to climb when leaving Winchester by east or west. The northern and eastern escarpments of the chalkland present several fine prominences, such as Beacon Hill skirted by the road north from Whitchurch and Cottington's Hill near Kingsclere. A noble stretch runs south to Langrish from Selborne and includes Stonor Hill, perhaps the most beautiful hill in all the county; here the road winds down a precipitous tree-lined ravine affording occasional glimpses of aptly-named Steep, near Petersfield. Looming against the skyline a few miles to the south is Butser Hill, termination of the South Downs Way and in appearance very typical of the huge beacons of the South Downs. Among the beech hangers clinging to the steep slopes of these hills the best-known is that at Selborne described in Gilbert White's writings. Yews grow vigorously on the chalk, and long shelter belts of mixed beech, yew and conifers are seen in places, sometimes around an exposed farm. From many high places on these uplands extensive views can be enjoyed over miles of quiet, well-kept countryside, the very picture of a land in good heart. There is a marvellous one at Cheesefoot Head on the Petersfield road just outside Winchester, where you can gaze over a vast tract of rolling farmland to the distant Solent shores; close by in the other direction is one of the most perfect grassy amphitheatres ever made by Nature.

All this Hampshire downland is splendid corn-growing country although some of it looks too flinty to grow anything much. Through the year it presents a changing picture, starting in spring with the first tentative shoots which quickly ripen to a richer green and lengthen with the days. By late July the huge fields are bronzing under the sun and ready for the combines to cut their wide swathes, leaving threadbare carpets of stubble behind them. Then comes baling or burning of the straw and sometimes eerie night scenes as the flames flicker across the fields like rows of campfires. With autumn ploughing the earthy underfelt is revealed, ready for sowing and the beginning of a fresh cycle.

Crossing over this chalk countryside and passing Winchester brings us to the third major landscape region, the Hampshire Basin, whose characteristic subsoils are clays, sands and gravels. This area occupies a rough triangle south and west of a line running from Mottisfont in the west to Rowlands Castle in the east; there is no obvious break with the downland chalk which dips gently to the south in contrast with its escarpment in the north. The largest part of this triangle is taken up by the New Forest, a landscape unique in western Europe which has been managed since Norman times, originally as a royal hunting preserve. It is by no means all trees—there are large areas of open heathland separating the 'ancient and ornamental' woods and plantations. Much planting of softwoods in the inclosures of the Forestry Commission has radically altered the character of some areas and been the cause of fierce controversy; indeed, this seems to be the result of almost any action in the Forest departing from established custom.

The New Forest is deservedly popular for it offers great freedom of movement and variety of scene. At no season of the year is it unappealing since it has both form and colour with which to please: and that colour includes not only all those one expects from trees but miles of purple heather in the late summer and rich blue distances where woods and plantations meet the sky. The Forest is a place of moods too, ranging from the tranquillity of a sunlit glade to the ferocity of a storm blasting the open heath with drenching sleet and rain.

Unfortunately, the eastern side of this region is a good deal less attractive since it comprises the Southampton and Portsmouth conurbation with its hinterland of sprawling settlements, busy roads and market gardens. It has one striking landscape feature, the bold chalk ridge of Portsdown, standing like a rampart behind Portsmouth, from which there are views of the city and harbour which you would have to be in a hurry not to find compelling.

Hampshire is intersected by four incomparable rivers, in their upper reaches chalk streams of a crystal purity it is a joy to behold: the Avon reaching the sea at Christchurch, the Test and Itchen flowing into upper

Southampton Water, the Meon entering it lower down. They provide some of the most charming scenery in the county, gliding through peaceful valleys and lush watermeadows where occasional plantations of poplars create a vertical accent. Above all, they are classic fly-fishermen's waters which have bred a host of famous anglers and their books and are now jealously protected. For that reason many of the river banks are not readily accessible and you must be content to follow their courses from the roads which conveniently follow them. Two routes are especially delightful. One, making a short trip from Winchester, lies along the upper Itchen valley and you could go up one bank, cross over and return by the other and have the satisfaction of seeing the three Worthys: Martyr, Abbot's and King's. A longer excursion is to follow the Test north from Romsey, preferably taking the lanes along the west bank and seeing a string of delectable villages, Houghton, Longstock, Wherwell, Longparish and Freefolk before eventually coming to Overton where the river rises. This is some of the best that Hampshire has to offer.

The county's coast, as mentioned before, is not of great scenic interest, being for the most part low-lying. Christchurch Bay, backed by fossil-rich clay cliffs, is popular with holidaymakers but elsewhere good bathing beaches are few. It is the sailing enthusiasts who are best catered for, with sheltered water and excellent harbourage at Keyhaven, Lymington, Beaulieu River, Hamble, Portsmouth and Langstone as well as Southampton Water itself.

The shape and scenery of the Isle of Wight are even more obviously related to the geological structure than is the mainland. Here it is a backbone of chalk running from Culver Cliff to the Needles that has produced the familiar lozenge shape of the island. To the north of it is subsoil and gentle scenery very much like the mainland to which it was once joined, to south a more complicated and hilly landscape lying between the chalk backbone and the Southern Downs. In fact, the island has a considerable range of scenery within a small compass, including marshy estuaries, woods, steep-banked lanes, open downland, rocky shores and majestic cliffs.

Despite the pressures created by urban and industrial developments, recreational demand and military needs, Hampshire and the Isle of Wight can show an astonishing wealth of wildlife which, far from struggling to maintain footholds is visibly flourishing; mild climate and moderate rainfall play a part in this. Like the scenery, it is closely related to the underlying structure and each of the regions already described has a typical flora and fauna.

Where the chalk downland has been left unploughed a rich and attractive flora is to be met with. Wild thyme makes a scented cushion underfoot and the yellow rockrose puts on a cheerful face; horseshoe vetch and scabious are found everywhere and cowslips and orchids occur locally. This is the habitat of the Chalkhill Blue which flits about like a kind of airborne forget-me-not. Partridge and pheasant abound, the latter having such poor road sense as to be a frequent hazard to motorists. Among the mammals of the downland rabbits and hares are on the increase while fallow deer are much more common in the large woods than may be realised. The beech hangers have their own particular plants like the large white helleborine and the birdsnest orchid.

The poor sandy soils of northeast Hampshire have a good deal in common with those of the south and southwest and are home to similar plants. Both have large areas of heathland and occasional sphagnum peat bogs where the unwary seeker after sundew and bog asphodel takes the risk of wet feet. The wild gladiolus, a great rarity, grows in the New Forest. It goes without saying that in the Forest trees are to be enjoyed in all their magnificence: native British oak and beech stand to full stature and many kinds of introduced softwoods grow either in plantations or as specimens. The Ornamental Drive near Lyndhurst and the Arboretum at Boldrewood with its huge redwoods are a tree-lover's delight. All the five kinds of deer which live in Britain are found in the forest: sika, roe, red, fallow (the most common) and muntjac (Chinese barking deer). Badgers are common though rarely seen. Butterflies, moths and other insects flourish.

Other kinds of habitat are to be found along the coast: mudflats in the sheltered waters of the Solent, and salt marshes in estuaries and harbours such as Langstone and Titchfield Haven. Farlington Marshes have a big population of Brent Geese and other duck. The interests of wildlife in Hampshire and the Isle of Wight are carefully watched by an active Trust which manages a series of reserves and sites of special interest.

It is less easy trying to match styles of building to the landscape than it is plants and animals for there are no materials or methods of construction confined to this region alone. The most eye-catching buildings (cathedrals, castles and country houses apart) are the timbered thatched cottages which survive in great numbers and are eagerly sought out by the well-to-do as weekend retreats and retirement homes; both mainland and island are thickly sprinkled with them. The thatching on these cottages deserves a special mention because so much, of such high quality is to be seen. Three basic kinds are practised. Long straw, typical of corn growing areas, has the appearance of a thick head of hair having been combed out on the roof. It is held down at the eaves and ridge with patterns of split hazel spars. Then there is Norfolk Reed which looks much crisper as the butt ends of the reeds are all beaten back in line with the roof slope; it has no eaves sparring. In recent years it has become much more common in Hampshire than it used to be, owing to the popularity of short-stalked varieties of wheat which have made long straw difficult to get. The third kind of thatch is combed wheat reed in which selected wheat straw is prepared to make something like a smaller Norfolk reed, and in use it is difficult to tell them apart. All thatched roofs may have decorative ridges where the thatcher's personal style comes out. You have only to drive round northwest Hampshire to see whole villages that prove how well the thatcher's craft is flourishing.

Another natural material extensively used in the region is flint, found in quantity on the downland and employed to build cottages, farmhouses, barns and churches; it must have helped to clear the fields a long time ago though modern deep ploughing has brought up a lot more since. Hampshire flint work seems to lack the precise neatness seen in Sussex and square-knapped flint work is rare, but the much-repaired wall of the Close at Winchester shows just how attractive this humble material can be. Because flint walls lack cohesion they are usually given brick quoins at corners and larger buildings may be bonded with many brick courses; sometimes the mellow old brickwork gives them an appearance reminiscent of faded striped jumpers. Squared stone blocks are often incorporated in walls of larger flint buildings for the same reason, sometimes closely enough to produce a chequered effect.

One rather uncommon material sometimes met with unexpectedly in older buildings is rammed chalk, which can be quite strong when properly done. A large barn or warehouse may have walls up to three feet thick and almost as hard as concrete. Farmyard and garden walls of chalk or chalk and clay are found in many places, neatly thatched or roofed with slates to keep out the wet which would destroy them.

Building stone is plentiful in the Isle of Wight, but in Hampshire it occurs only in a small area on the eastern side of the county where the greensand of the Sussex weald crosses the border. It is met with in rocky road cuttings overhung by trees and in outcrops along streams and it has produced some villages of distinctive character such as Selborne and Buriton. The stone is grey or of brownish tinge when there is iron in it, and it is used in smallish irregular pieces as though too scarce to waste; only the more important houses are built of coursed stone.

When we turn from the countryside to look at the towns we find a great variety, and a surprising number on the mainland for one county: more than a dozen, ranging from a compact little place like New Alresford (which would probably prefer to call itself a village) to sprawling Southampton and crowded Portsmouth. Nearly all are of a respectable antiquity, some are very old indeed and few of them could be held dull.

Southampton does not give of its best to the traveller hurrying to catch a boat or grinding his way along the coastal route, but a drive in from Winchester will take you past a green suburb, through the Common and into a town centre spacious and charmingly gardened. It is a phoenix town, terribly devastated by wartime bombing, that has made a successful effort to efface the old scars. Walking round it is pleasant, with glimpses on the west side of liner funnels in the docks and unexpected encounters with its ancient past. The city takes pride in its surviving old buildings, mostly open to the public as museums, and in the fine stretches of its old walls. Wartime damage has had an interesting side-effect in making large areas of the medieval town available for archaeological investigation and there is usually something of the work to be looked at in the summer months.

Not far away, and almost joined by the developments of modern times, is Portsmouth, also very dependent on the sea. Though it has some resort facilities at Southsea it is not generally thought of as a tourist town; but in this near-island there is a great deal to see. The chief areas of interest are in Old Portsmouth and the Dockyard. The former was once a very seedy cosmopolitan area within the old defences and has all sorts of intriguing corners now smartened up after wartime destruction. Access to the Dockyard is necessarily restricted except for visiting HMS *Victory* and the nearby museum, which is a pity as some of the older buildings have considerable architectural merit and are of interest to the enthusiast in industrial history. Just a short ferry ride across the harbour is Gosport: not obviously an attractive place but with all sorts of naval and military associations and some barrack buildings that are now seen as having a certain merit. The whole area of Portsmouth Harbour is packed with activity and a ferry trip to Ryde will take you past all sorts of interesting shipping and sights.

The one town to which every visitor goes without fail is Winchester – and rightly so. 'If Hampshire had no other history but Winchester it would be enough. It is the unequalled town . . .' wrote Arthur Mee, and few would wish to deny it. For this small city has a special quality and an atmosphere compounded of things belonging to the provincial way of life: a bustling High Street, quiet bookshops, gracious old buildings, sweeping lawns, college boys in straw boaters, elderly clergymen in the Close, country people getting off buses, and over all that serenity which life somehow acquires when lived within the shadow of a great cathedral. The place is steeped in history. Tourists from every nation flock to this epitome of Englishness and it remains quite unspoiled.

Of Hampshire's smaller towns the most appealing are probably Lymington, New Alresford, Romsey and Petersfield. Each retains a good deal of its market town flavour, each has an air of tidy respectability. For sheer immaculate neatness Alresford's Broad Street is hard to match; Romsey, huddled in the shelter of its abbey has a kind of cosyness that is quite different from Petersfield with its spacious market place fronting the church; Lymington is a busy ferry terminal and sailing centre with an air of holiday relaxation about it.

The other towns are somewhat workaday places where you will not linger for long unless you know the quiet satisfaction of watching ordinary people going about their ordinary affairs as they have done time out of mind: Alton, Andover and Ringwood are such towns. Each has a weekly market which shows the place at its most interesting. Stout countrywomen and men with weatherbeaten faces scour the stalls for cheap offers and clog the pavements chatting to acquaintances. The auctioneer stands on a broken chair in the nearby saleground and makes his well-worn witticisms at the expense of old motor mowers and tight-fisted bidders. In the row of cages ducks look at you with anxious cocked heads and rabbits chew on placidly, careless of the two lithe ferrets in the compartment below. If you're looking for sweet pea plants, cut-price groceries or a bargain antique, this is the place. Whatever these towns may be on other days of the week, they are far from dull on market days.

It is, unfortunately, hard to say much about the remaining towns. Aldershot has few graces, but much military history and several service museums; it runs imperceptibly into neighbouring Farnborough, whose time of glory is the biennial air show. The town does, however, have one utterly-unexpected and little-known feature: the mausoleum of Napoleon III at St. Michael's Abbey. Here in a crypt of solemn marble are the tombs of the Emperor, his wife Eugènie (who spent her widowhood in the town) and their son the Prince Imperial, killed while serving with the British army in the Zulu War. There is, alas, even less to be said for Basingstoke – once a small market and industrial town of plain but honest character, now a poor shadow of its former self, re-planned out of recognition and surrounded by a strangulating system of ringroads.

In these words of introduction there has only been space to give an outline picture of Hampshire and the Isle of Wight for the benefit of those who are new to their delights. Little has been said about history or churches or special events, for this is not a guidebook; it is intended to inspire appreciation, and if it succeeds in doing that it will send the reader searching out for himself more of the good things to be enjoyed in the area. It may, for instance, set him on the trail of the writers who have lived and found inspiration here; it may encourage expeditions to the prehistoric hillforts and along the tracks of Roman roads; or it may lead to discovery of the folklore surrounding the unassuming lives of people in quiet villages. It may, best of all, lead him to a discovery of the underlying peace of this special part of England.

PONIES OF THE NEW FOREST

The wiry little ponies have an engaging way of dominating one's memories of a visit to the Forest, though great numbers of cattle also graze there. They can be placed in two groups by habit: those who feed in the open forest and those who feed on the verges. It is the latter who cause the traffic hazards, sometimes intensified by the innocent foolhardiness of foals who have a liking for sleeping on the warm road surface itself. Long stretches of the main roads have now been fenced as a counter measure.

Little is known about the origins of the ponies who back in Norman times were referred to as 'wild horses'. Attempts over the centuries to improve the stock have had little result and the basic type continues, tough, hardy, sharp-witted and of many colours. Strictly speaking they are not wild for all are owned and listed in the New Forest Pony Studbook and there is an annual roundup and sale at Beaulieu Road Station. Hard winters may appear to treat them unkindly, but as long as they can get heather, brambles, gorse tops or holly they have a good chance of surviving.

QUAY HILL, LYMINGTON

Lymington is a pretty place to which most New Forest visitors gravitate sooner or later; it makes an excellent centre for a variety of excursions, with Christchurch, Beaulieu, Buckler's Hard, Hurst Castle and the Isle of Wight all within convenient reach. The High Street falls steeply to Quay Hill, at the bottom of which is an irresistible turning leading to Town Quay, lively with small-boat activity and sailing people (stroll downstream to the huge marina if you want to gaze at the style and splendour of the larger boats). There is a long tradition of boatbuilding in Lymington and one boatyard is still turning out quite large wooden vessels, building up keel, stem, sternpost, frames and planking in the centuries-old way. It is impressive craftsmanship.

A stroll up the High Street will take you past neat shops that look as if they are still run by people, past some neat eighteenth-century houses to St Thomas's Church whose cupola draws the eye from down the street. In Church Lane nearby are two unusual crinkle-crankle walls with sinuous curves designed to lend strength to their thin fabric.

MEW'S
Three
Quay
Hill

PALACE HOUSE, BEAULIEU

Despite being one of the most-visited corners of the New Forest with its stately home and Motor Museum, Beaulieu manages to remain the *beautiful place* that it was when the Cistercian monks settled here in 1204; when they began to build their great abbey they must have found all the solitude they could want. For 300 years it stood, until the day in 1538 when the abbot and 20 monks 'by unanimous consent did give, grant, render and confirm the monastery . . . to our illustrious prince and lord, Henry VIII'. It was purchased by Thomas Wriothesley and used as a quarry to build Calshott and Hurst Castles as defences against the French.

Four parts of the abbey remain. The Outer Gatehouse faces Beaulieu village and leads to the Great Gatehouse of early fourteenth-century date. Extensive additions were made to it in the 1870s and it is now known as Palace House. The *domus conversorum* or Dormitory of the lay brothers serves as a pleasant restaurant and the monks' Refectory has become the parish church. This accounts for the unusual north-south alignment and the elegant reading pulpit in one wall from which one of the monks would have read to the brethren at mealtimes.

NATIONAL MOTOR MUSEUM, BEAULIEU

Kipling's dictum, 'transportation is civilisation' could well be the philosophy of this stimulating exhibition. For the National Motor Museum is undoubtedly a shrine to one of the moving passions of the twentieth century, which may help to explain the remarkable speed with which its collections have grown. It was only 20 years after Lord Montagu founded the collection in the hall of his home, Palace House, that the present building was opened in 1972. Now it contains one of the most comprehensive assemblages of historic vehicles anywhere, with sections for veteran, vintage and post-vintage, record-breaking, racing and sports cars, commercial vehicles and motorcycles. There is also a comprehensive research library on the history of the motor industry.

Behind the Ford GT 40 Mk 3 in the foreground enthusiasts may recognise a pretty 1912 Hispano-Suiza *Alfonso XIII* (named after a king of Spain who was given one for his birthday in 1909), and in the background the aerodynamic hull of Donald Campbell's £1 million *Bluebird*. The cars in the collection date from 1895 onwards, telling within the lifespan of some visitors a story of astonishing technological progress.

Despite its size and striking design the Museum and its facilities have been almost entirely concealed in the natural landscape, a creditable example of how these things can be done.

Please do not
touch exhibits
Shell
FGC 409
LLP 798
SPP 604D
OHP
43

BUCKLER'S HARD

It is difficult to imagine that this placid stretch of the Beaulieu River was once a thriving shipyard, and even more difficult to envisage the hamlet of Buckler's Hard as a major port, though such was the unrealised ambition of John, 2nd Duke of Montagu when he began to build it in 1724; he intended it to be a base for his proposed sugar trade with the West Indies. When war with France broke out in 1740 there came an increased demand for shipbuilding sites and the hamlet took on a new role. A long line of naval and merchant vessels was built here, mostly by Henry Adams and his sons, bearing such proud names as *Vigilant, Indefatigable* and *Illustrious,* rating up to 74 guns; among them was *Agamemnon,* Nelson's favourite ship.

By the middle of last century shipbuilding had declined at Buckler's Hard as wooden ships gave way to iron and steel; however, it enjoyed a brief but vital revival during the 1939–45 war. Henry Adams' house at one end of the two brick terraces sloping down to the river is now an hotel, and the former Sun Inn an informative Maritime Museum where the story of the settlement is told.

AUTUMN IN THE FOREST

The New Forest has always been a very special part of Hampshire. Parts of it were royal forest before the Norman conquest but it was William I who ordered its afforestation in 1079 to satisfy his passion for hunting and he protected his interests vigorously. Cruel penalties were meted out to any man foolish enough to disturb the deer, or worse still, to kill one. In later years the royal prerogatives were weakened by many claims upon the Forest lands and resources, culminating in huge demands for shipbuilding timber during Elizabeth I's reign and the late eighteenth century when Britain was vieing for command of the seas. Today the New Forest is under great pressure for recreational use and is the subject of a vigorous conservation lobby.

Forest law, enforced by the Verderers' Court and its Agisters, is a fascinating business. Ancient Rights of Common are still available to those living on land to which they pertain: Common of Pasture for Commonable Animals (ponies, horses, cattle and donkeys), Common of Mast (for grazing pigs), Common of Pasture (for sheep), Common of Turbary (cutting turf for fuel), Common of Marl (digging marl for fertiliser) and Common of Estovers (cutting firewood); only the first two are still much exercised.

THE TEST AT ROMSEY

Most people go to Romsey to see the Abbey, a glorious pile begun *c.* 970 on the site of a nunnery built by the Saxon King Edward the Elder for his daughter Elfleda. Most of what we see today was completed by the thirteenth century and would have been destroyed at the Dissolution of the monasteries had the town not stepped in and bought the building for a parish church. Among the lovely things in the Abbey are two notable pieces of sculpture, the older in the south chancel being a crucifixion group of Anglo-Saxon date. The other is outside, on the west wall of the south transept: the early eleventh-century Romsey Rood portraying Christ stiffly erect on the cross while the hand of God reaches down out of a curly cloud in blessing.

For many others Romsey means first and foremost the River Test and all the associations that go with some of the world's most revered and coveted waters. Along them generations of sportsmen have studied the ways of the fly and striven to emulate her with alluring likenesses. Some famous flies have been tied on this river and names like the *Houghton Ruby* and *Lunn's Particular* preserve chapters of its angling history.

ST. MARY THE LESS, CHILBOLTON

Chilbolton is one of the pleasant villages sprinkled along the delectable Test Valley north of Romsey. It is typical of many Hampshire villages today, being chiefly dwelt in by commuters but still managing to retain plenty of those things which seem to make village life more desirable than ever: a cricket team, women's institute, church fête, village pub, jumble sales in aid of this and that, and the cosy gossip of a small community.

In the church – mostly thirteenth- and fourteenth-century work – the chief point of interest is the Jacobean pulpit with linenfold panelling. Hard by, an early eighteenth-century rectory preserves a mellow dignity, suitably aloof from other houses.

The village is blessed with two open spaces that attract many weekend visitors: West Down, where the cowslip, meadow saxifrage and purple danesblood grow and where paths afford surprise views of the curving Test; and the Common which extends across two branches of the same river. Here the picnickers come on summer Sunday afternoons and village children dive in the deep pools. A long footbridge spans the farthest stream where bright-eyed mallard vie for breadcrumbs and speckled trout lie in the flowing waterweed or leap with a silver flash for unwary mayflies.

EAST MEON

Nestling under a smooth knoll of downland is this village of considerable charm with a stream flowing down its High Street and warm old brick and thatch. There is a working forge, and near the church an ancient Court House of the Bishops of Winchester. The church stands on rising ground surrounded by old trees, its spire stabbing the skyline from a noble Norman tower; within, the stonework is massive and strong, much of it of similar early date.

There is one treasure inside for which alone it would be worth visiting – the great square font of black Tournai marble. Two sides are carved with shallow arcading and birds and beasts, two with scenes from the story of Adam and Eve. We are shown the creation of the man and his partner, then their temptation, Eve receiving an apple from the serpent's mouth. The paradise from which they are subsequently expelled is seen as a city with splendid arcaded buildings before which stands the angel with sword. Lastly, the angel has taken a spade to show Adam how to till the soil, while Eve is already spinning with her distaff. The figures are squat, almond-eyed and grave, telling their story with timeless dramatic effect.

IND COOPE
THE GEORGE
POST OFFICE STORES

WINCHESTER CATHEDRAL

Surrounded by green lawns and ancient trees, the Cathedral Church of St. Swithun is a magnet for visitors from all over the world. Famous now as the longest church in Europe, it was a much more modest affair when the Old Minster was founded in the mid-7th century; its remains lie to the north of the present nave. The interior is a glorious panoply of styles; the transepts, brooding and fortress-like, show how the nave of 1079 must have looked before a Perpendicular facelift created the present majestic vista.

The building is rich with memories of the famous. A cardinal and six bishops lie in the beautiful chantry chapels; all but one were Chancellors of England. One of them is William of Wykeham who founded both Winchester College and New College, Oxford. In mortuary chests above the Presbytery rest the bones of Saxon kings, Edmund and Ethelwulf and Canute; William Rufus is in the Choir. Henry IV and Joan of Navarre were married in the Cathedral, and so were Mary I and Philip of Spain. In the Retrochoir is a small statue of the man to whom many will feel especially grateful: William Walker, the diver who saved the building by spending six years underpinning it with his own hands.

TOWN MILL, WINCHESTER

Winchester is full of delights for anyone who can appreciate the sense of history which pervades it, for it has been liberally endowed with mellow old buildings and associations with the great and famous. In Saxon times this was the capital of England; the Norman kings had their treasury here, and William the Conqueror built a palace. Charles II planned an ambitious one which never got beyond the first stage.

At the top of High Street is the Great Hall of the Norman castle, best known for its fifteenth-century Round Table, where Richard the Lion-heart was greeted by the nobles on his return from captivity, and Sir Walter Raleigh tried for his life. From nearby Westgate is a splendid view of High Street and St Giles Hill. Beyond King Alfred's statue at the bottom of the street is the Town Mill, and a stone's throw further, the half-timbered Old Chesil Rectory. Naturally, you will find your way to the Cathedral and the College, but search out some of the quiet corners also, like the tiny church of St. Swithun upon Kingsgate, and above all, make a pilgrimage to the lovely Hospital of St Cross whose brethren are often to be seen in the streets in their gowns of mulberry and black.

BARGATE, SOUTHAMPTON

It has aptly been described as looking 'like a piece of huge stage scenery' since being cut off from its adjacent walls, but for all that Bargate is one of the finest town gateways in Britain; the earliest part was probably built before 1200, most of it two centuries later. On this south side are the watch bell and an incongruous figure of George III in Roman garb. In medieval times the upper floor was used as the Guildhall and is now a museum relating to the town's history. Bargate has the distinction of being one of two places in England where carols are sung on May morning – though you will have to be up early to hear them before the traffic is about.

This is a good place to begin a circuit of the old walls of which substantial sections have somehow survived both wartime bombing and postwar development. A walk along them to the west (the best stretch) will bring you to West Quay from which the *Mayflower* and *Speedwell* sailed in 1620, past the Pilgrim Fathers Memorial to two well-restored buildings: the Wool House (fourteenth century) and God's House Tower (fifteenth century) housing respectively the Maritime and the Archaeological Museums.

AT SOUTHAMPTON DOCKS

Southampton's history as a great international port began with a Roman settlement on the Itchen estuary. It was followed by a Saxon trading post known in later years as Hamtun which gave its name to the region, Hamtunscire. To the Normans the port was a vital cross-channel link and they fortified it suitably; when the links with Normandy were broken it became the object of a number of raids and burnings by the French. An easy overland route to London encouraged the development of extensive trade in the middle ages and finds made in the excavations of recent years show regular contact with the Mediterranean.

Better ships in Tudor times meant easier sailing to London and the town went into a decline. In the early nineteenth century it began to find new life as a spa and resort town, but it was the arrival of the railway and subsequent expansion of the docks which restored it to pre-eminence as a port; the great days of the liner terminal reached their climax in 1933 with the opening of the King George V Graving Dock, big enough to take the *Queen Mary*. The growth of air travel has brought further changes and the docks have been extensively developed to cope with container traffic.

BENARMIN
LEITH

OUTSIDE THE WALLS OF PORTCHESTER

Portchester Castle is one of the most impressive ancient monuments in Hampshire, preserving as it does almost the entire circuit of its Roman walls 20 feet high and ten feet broad. It is one of a series of forts built in the third century AD to protect the channel coast against Saxon pirates and its survival says much for the strength of its flint walls bonded with courses of tile and stone. Excavation has shown that after the departure of the Romans it was occasionally occupied in Saxon times, and then, in 1133, Henry I founded a small Augustinian priory in one corner. Its duration was short, but one building survives in use as the parish church of St Mary's, a fine example of Romanesque style.

The medieval castle of which the keep is such a conspicuous part was built in the opposite corner to the priory in the middle of the twelfth century; it partly incorporated the Roman walls and made use of them as an outer bailey. Its history seems to have been a quiet one, highlighted by the embarkation of various monarchs for the Continent, among them Henry V on his way to Agincourt. Sundry graffiti on the walls testify to the presence of French prisoners during the Napoleonic wars.

PORTSMOUTH CATHEDRAL

It was not until 1927 that the parish church of St Thomas became the Cathedral and progressive enlargement since then has given it an appearance which belies its age; it dates from the twelfth century. The tower is its most striking external feature. In the middle ages it was used as a naval watch-tower and lantern, and during the Civil War as an observation post, drawing damaging fire from Cromwell's artillery in Gosport. The bell cupola and ship weathervane were put on in Queen Anne's reign.

The Cathedral stands at the heart of Old Portsmouth, an area interesting for the elaborate defences whose construction was begun by Charles II to protect the harbour mouth and the Camber inlet. Most of them were demolished a century ago when new defensive strategy was developed based on a chain of forts on the town's outskirts, but an interesting series of towers and walls survives along the south-western shore. You can follow their line from the Round Tower past the Eighteen Gun Battery and the Saluting Platform to King's Bastion; further on you come to Southsea Castle, carefully restored and now housing collections illustrating the military and maritime history of Portsmouth.

THE EDGE OF OLD PORTSMOUTH

Here is a part of Point, the curious little peninsula belonging to Old Portsmouth. In the left background is Quebec House, built by public subscription in 1754 as a bathing house, with the harbour beyond. Point (whose inhabitants used to be known as *Spice Islanders*) once had a quite remarkable reputation which cannot be better appreciated than through the words of a local historian describing its main throughfare, Broad Street, in 1801:

'This street is filled with one of the most heterogeneous assemblages of traffic and conviviality that is, perhaps, to be found in the same extent in any one street, and in any one part of the world. Liquor shops, contract taverns, Jew shopmen, tailors and drapers jostle Christian pawnbrokers, watch jobbers and trinket merchants; cook-shops, eating houses and ordinaries vie with each other to entertain all classes, from the guests of the cabin to those of the forecastle, and whilst honest and hearty Jack is dancing with his favourite girl in the lower decks of a liquor shop, his respectable superiors are enjoying aloft, in the room of a tavern, the fruits of their bravery, in that style of elegance their distinguished talents and characters so eminently merit.'

HMS *VICTORY*

Portsmouth is privileged to be the resting place of this noble ship, immortalised by the events of one day, 21 October 1805 when Nelson died aboard her in the hour of victory. In fact, she already had an honourable career behind her and had been the flagship of many other admirals. *Victory* was six years building, cost over £57,000 and then had to wait 13 years for her first commission in 1778. She spent the last two years of the eighteenth century at Chatham as a hospital ship for prisoners, and it was in the subsequent refit that she took on her present appearance. Nelson had the gun decks of all his ships painted with an ochre band and the topsides between and the outsides of the port lids painted black, so producing a characteristic chequered appearance when closed.

Victory last saw active service in 1813 and was finally brought out of the water in 1922. With one break she has been the flagship of Portsmouth Command since 1824 and is regularly used for official functions. Visitors will find an extensive collection of Nelsoniana and a panorama of the action at Trafalgar at its height in the nearby Royal Naval Museum.

LANGSTONE HARBOUR

If you can appreciate a landscape of lonely flatnesses and expansive sky then you will enjoy the quiet appeal of Langstone Harbour. At high tide it is a great reed-fringed stretch of shallow water, often an intense blue; at low tide it is a desolation of mud intersected by narrow gleaming channels. The tiny settlement of Langstone lies at the head of the harbour, approached by a channel lying between two spits, the East and West Winners; today it is a smart little retreat for weekend sailors, but in the past it had a life and business all its own as the port for Havant. The coming of the railway began to change all that and the last coaling schooner to tie up at the quayside has become a distant memory.

The fifteenth-century Royal Oak Inn was once a haunt of the smugglers for which this area was notorious; submerged floating rafts were used as a means of concealing contraband in the harbour. Next to the inn are the remains of the unusual combined tide- and wind-mill. Langstone used to be well-known for its oysters and in the middle of last century some 50 sail were dredging here and in neighbouring Chichester Harbour.

ROYAL OAK
ODS
THE ROYAL OAK
FULLY LICENSED

IN GILBERT WHITE'S VILLAGE

How a village as much visited as Selborne can manage to remain unspoiled is something of a marvel, unless it is that those who go there mostly share Gilbert White's concern for the countryside. Had he never lived here this view of the Plestor outside the church would be no less pretty, but to walk along the self-same paths, climb the zig-zag that he built up the Hanger and see the limes that he planted to screen off the butcher's shop is to share for a while the village he knew and whose natural history he recorded so diligently. At his home, The Wakes (much added to since his day), you may step into the parlour where he wrote and walk down the little brick path he made across his lawn, thankful that all is so sympathetically cared for. It is appropriate that a small field-study centre has recently been opened in the grounds.

Gilbert White was curate of nearby Faringdon and then Selborne for 32 years until his death and his well-used sermon notes show that he was also a man of duty. When he died he was buried on the north side of the church beneath a characteristically unassuming headstone that is only identified by the letters G.W.

JANE AUSTEN'S HOUSE AT CHAWTON

There is something about this neat, unpretentious house that seems particularly fitting to Miss Austen, that serene observer of human relationships. She moved here in 1809 with her mother and sister Cassandra after her father's death; he was rector at Steventon near Basingstoke where she was born and lived for 25 years. Evidently the house pleased her for she expressed her feelings about it in a letter to her brother:

Our Chawton house, how much we find
Already in it to our mind:
And how convinced, that when complete
It will all other houses beat.

Care has been taken to return it to much the same appearance it must have had in Jane's time, and we can inspect the drawing room where she practised the piano before breakfast and the dining room where she did her writing. It was in this house that she wrote *Mansfield Park, Emma* and *Persuasion* and rewrote her other great novels. It has been furnished with several pieces of family furniture and odds and ends associated with the authoress.

Jane Austen spent her last few weeks at the house marked with a plaque in College Street, Winchester where she died in July 1817.

JANE
AUSTENS
HOUSE

THE VYNE

Hampshire is not over-endowed with great houses and this is the finest of them, recognised long ago by John Leland as 'one of the principal houses in goodly building in all Hamptonshire'. The walls of diapered brickwork are Tudor in date, the north portico (seen here) mid-seventeenth century. On the upper floor of the west front is one of the most beautiful features of the early period, the Long Gallery lined with intricate linenfold panelling. Henry VIII and Catherine of Aragon visited the house in 1510 and are portrayed in the Flemish glass of the Chapel. In the splendid Tomb Chamber next door is a monument to Chaloner Chute who bought the estate in 1653. He became Speaker of the House of Commons in 1659, died the same year and is portrayed in his robes lying on a straw mat.

While at the Vyne it is easy to visit the Roman town of Calleva which lies beneath the fields of Silchester three miles to the north. The walls, still standing in part, enclosed a civilised town which had a grid of streets, a spacious forum, a large official guest house or *mansio* and a tiny Christian church. An amphitheatre outside the walls on the east provided entertainment.

OSBORNE – ROYAL RETREAT

Early in their married life the young Queen Victoria and her husband felt the need of 'a place of one's own, quiet and retired' as she put it, where they could escape the public eye. After the purchase of an estate in the Isle of Wight the Prince Consort (aided by the architect Thomas Cubitt) began to design Osborne House in Italianate style inspired, it is said, by a fancied resemblance of the Solent to the Bay of Naples. The couple first occupied the house in September 1846 and spent many of their happiest years here. It was here that Victoria retired after Albert's death in 1861, and here that she died in 1901. She kept everything just as Albert left it, and so it remains today.

Osborne is full of things illustrating the taste of the period: there is the Horn Room whose furniture is made from antlers, and the massive billiard table with painted designs by Albert. There are also many reminders of the happy life enjoyed at Osborne: the Queen's bathing machine, the Swiss cottage built for the royal children, the miniature fort built by Prince Arthur (later a Field Marshal), and a series of marble models of the children's limbs.

GODSHILL, THE PICTURE VILLAGE

In its setting of leafy lanes with neatly-thatched cottages and gardens rich with flowers Godshill epitomises 'the garden isle'; yet its very prettiness is almost its undoing for the place tries so hard to satisfy the visitor that its essential rural simplicity is easily overlooked. If tea and postcards are not your only end in visiting Godshill then a look round the parish church is probably the most satisfying thing to do and there are several interesting features to see.

A fine group of monuments commemorates the Worsley family, one of whom, Sir James, was Master of the Robes to Henry VIII and responsible for organising the Field of the Cloth of Gold; a tilting helmet hangs over the canopy beneath which he and his wife kneel. Then there is the beautiful tomb of Sir John Leigh and his wife Agnes, upon the soles of whose feet are carved little weeping figures. A fifteenth-century wall-painting showing Christ crucified on a lily spray is unique in England. Outside, among quaint specimens of rustic churchyard art, is the grave of Bartholomew Jacobs with this couplet, calculated to send the beholder away in thoughtful mood:

Man is the seed; God is the sower;
Man is the grass. Death is the mower.

SHANKLIN

Sheltering beneath the high cliffs of Shanklin Down this much-favoured resort enjoys a pleasant combination of seaside virtues and open downland close by. There are plenty of gardens with masses of hydrangeas in their season. Shanklin is a place of quite recent development which in 1846 could be described as 'very small and scattery'. That little village which Keats knew when he stayed in a cottage below the cliff is now much admired for its trimly-thatched houses and the elaborately carved bargeboards on their gables. To the north of it grew up the Victorian part whose villas, hotels and boarding houses have a rich period flavour which many see as the essential charm of the place.

On the southern side of the town lies its best-known feature, Shanklin Chine, a flowery, ferny ravine some 180 ft wide and 300 ft deep down which a zigzag path follows the cascading stream. Luccombe Chine, a mile further on, is reached by a clifftop path, and beyond that is the Landslip. In this dramatic feature the softer strata have slipped away towards the sea leaving harder cliffs exposed behind them. Gnarled trees and ferns grow among the rocks and there are steps giving access for the energetic to the woods below.